W9-BLA-915

Abe Lincoln was president from 1861 to 1865.

Abraham Lincoln was our 16th **president**. But he was a lot of other things, too. Turn the page to learn about this amazing man.

Abe was born in Kentucky in 1809. He lived in a log cabin. He loved the outdoors and sometimes wore a fur cap with a raccoon tail!

Abe worked to help his family earn money. He went to school for only a few weeks each year.

Abe grew tall and strong. During his life, he had many jobs. His first one was chopping wood for 25 cents a day. He was ten years old.

Abe made all the customers laugh with his funny stories.

As a young man, Abe drove a boat and was a soldier. He also worked in a general store. It sold different kinds of things, such as axes, spoons, and candy.

Throughout his life, Abe often wore a "stovepipe hat" like this one.

Abe also worked as a farmer and a postmaster. He would stick letters in his hat and walk many miles to give people their mail.

Abe always loved to read.

Abe decided he wanted to be a **lawyer**. Back then, there were only a few law schools. So he taught himself by reading books. It worked! Abe soon became a great lawyer.

Abe's sons sometimes came by his office to play.

In 1842, Abe married Mary Todd. Soon they started a family. Abe loved to play with his sons.

Abe was great at giving speeches.

During his years as a lawyer, Abe also worked in the state government of Illinois. He wanted to make America a better place to live.

Abe grew his famous beard right before he became president.

People called Abe "Honest Abe" because he was so **trustworthy**. "Honest Abe, why don't you run for president?" they said. So he did. And, in 1860, he won.

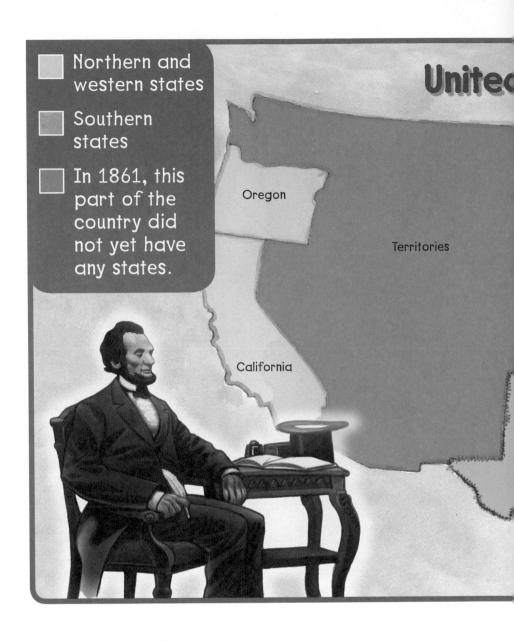

Northern and western states

Southern states

In 1861, this part of the country did not yet have any states.

Unite

Oregon

Territories

California

Being president was a hard job.
At that time, the United States had
big problems.

The southern states wanted to break away. They wanted to make their own country and continue to own **slaves**.

Abe disagreed. He thought America should stay together. He also thought slavery was very wrong. In 1861, the southern states attacked the northern states. This started the **Civil War**.

More than three million people fought in the war.

The Civil War lasted four years. Many battles were fought. Many lives were lost. But, in 1865, Abe Lincoln's army won.

When the war was over, people came to the White House and cheered for Abe.

America stayed together. In 1865, an important law was passed that freed all the slaves.

You can visit the Lincoln Memorial in Washington, D.C.

On Presidents' Day, we honor Abraham Lincoln. He was a great speaker and lawyer. But most of all, he was a great leader.

Glossary

Civil War (noun) the United States war between southern and northern states, which lasted from 1861 to 1865

lawyer (noun) a person who gives people advice about the law and speaks for them in court

master (noun) a person who owns slaves

president (noun) the person chosen by Americans to run the country

slave (noun) a person who is owned by another person

trustworthy (adjective) honest and reliable